JAN 0 2

SO-AGT-199

02092 4084

Animals of the World

Ocelot

By Edana Eckart

Welcome
Books™

Children's Press®
A Division of Scholastic Inc.
New York / Toronto / London / Auckland / Sydney
Mexico City / New Delhi / Hong Kong
Danbury, Connecticut

Photo Credits: Cover © Erwin & Peggy Bauer/Animals Animals; p. 5 © Buddy Mays/Corbis; p. 7 © Philip Perry; Frank Lane Picture Agency/Corbis; pp. 9, 11 © John Pontier/Animals Animals; p. 13 © Boyle&Boyle/Animals Animals; p. 15 © Peter Oxford/Nature Picture Library; p. 17 © David Aubrey/Corbis; p. 19 © Michael Dick/Animals Animals; p. 21 © Mc Donald Wildlife Photography/ Animals Animals
Contributing Editor: Jennifer Silate
Book Design: Mindy Liu

Library of Congress Cataloging-in-Publication Data

Eckart, Edana.
    Ocelot / by Edana Eckart.
    v. cm.—(Animals of the world)
    Contents: Cats—Living in forests—Hunting.
    ISBN 0-516-24297-0 (lib. bdg.)—ISBN 0-516-27894-0 (pbk.)
    1. Ocelot—Juvenile literature. [1. Ocelot.] I. Title.

    QL737.C23E345 2003
    599.75'2—dc21

                                                        2002154958

Contents

Ocelots are cats.

Ocelots have very pretty **fur**.

Their fur has many spots.

The spots help the ocelots hide.

7

Many ocelots live in **forests**.

Ocelots can **climb** trees in forests.

Ocelots like to play in water.

11

Ocelots sleep a lot.

They sleep for most
of the day.

13

Ocelots can see very well.

They can **hunt** for food at night.

Ocelots eat other animals, like mice.

Ocelot babies are called **kittens**.

Ocelot mothers take care of the kittens.

Ocelots are very beautiful animals.

New Words

climb (**klime**) to move up something using your
hands and feet

forests (**for**-ists) large areas where many trees
and other plants grow close together

fur (**fur**) soft, thick hair that covers the body of
some animals

hunt (**huhnt**) to search for other animals for food

kittens (**kit**-uhnz) baby cats

ocelots (**oss**-uh-lots) wild cats of medium size
with spotted fur

To Find Out More

Web Sites

Kid's Planet: Ocelot
http://www.kidsplanet.org/factsheets/ocelot.html
This Web site has lots of interesting information about ocelots.

Oakland Zoo: Ocelot
http://www.oaklandzoo.org/atoz/azocelot.html
Learn what ocelots eat, where they live, and more on this Web site.

Ocelot
http://www.pbs.org/kratts/world/sa/ocelot/index.html
Read about the ocelot and learn many interesting facts on this informative Web site.

Index

About the Author
Edana Eckart has written several children's books. She enjoys bike riding with her family.

Reading Consultants

Kris Flynn, Coordinator, Small School District Literacy, The San Diego County Office of Education

Shelly Forys, Certified Reading Recovery Specialist, W.J. Zahnow Elementary School, Waterloo, IL

Sue McAdams, Former President of the North Texas Reading Council of the IRA, and Early Literacy Consultant, Dallas, TX